The Gospel According to Jesus

Unwrapping Centuries of Confusion

Marc Carrier

"The Gospel According to Jesus: Unwrapping Centuries of Confusion" by Marc Carrier. Copyright © 2010, 2014 Marc Carrier.

You may use, translate, print and publish this material, in its entirety, without prior permission and without exclusive rights, in any language, for any people group, in any country for the following limited purposes: KINGDOM EXPANSION or EDIFICATION OF THE SAINTS. Copying, distribution, or dissemination of these materials, in whole or in part, for commercial purposes or for critique is expressly prohibited.

If you translate this book in any other language, please include the copyright statement from this page, so that no one can legally hinder its distribution, and also please inform the publisher at info@KingdomDriven.org so that the materials may be made available to others.

Scripture taken from the NEW AMERICAN STANDARD BIBLE®, Copyright © 1960, 1962, 1963, 1968, 1971, 1972, 1973, 1975, 1977, 1995 by The Lockman Foundation. Used by permission.

Additional print copies of this book and other materials by the author may be obtained through www.ValuesDrivenFamily.com and a free e-copy of this book and many other practical kingdom expansion resources may be obtained at www.KingdomDriven.org.

Table of Contents

- Foreword 5
- Introduction 7
- Problem…and Solution 9
- The Right Foundation 13
- Justice or Mercy 17
- The Kingdom of God 21
- Citizens of the Kingdom 25
- Dress Code 29
- Filthy Rags? 33
- Final Analysis 47

Foreword

For centuries, most churches have been preaching a message of "easy-believism." Just say a short prayer and invite Jesus into your heart, and you will be born again as a result. Heaven is absolutely guaranteed to you. (At least, that's what we're told.) It's not hard to see why churches preaching this easy gospel have no problem making lots of converts. But is this really the gospel that Jesus preached?

If today's gospel of easy-believism is authentic, then why did Jesus tell His apostles, "He who has My commandments and keeps them, it is he who loves Me. And he who loves Me will be loved by My Father, and I will love him" (John 14:21). That certainly sounds like being a true Christian involves more than having said the "sinner's prayer" at some time in your life. An obedient love-faith relationship with Jesus Christ is also required.

In *The Gospel According to Jesus: Unwrapping Centuries of Confusion*, Marc Carrier sets forth in a clear manner the historic gospel of Christianity. This is the gospel that Jesus preached, and it's the gospel that the early Christians preached. It's part of the "faith which was once for all delivered to the saints" (Jude 3). Although Marc sets forth this gospel in a succinct manner, everything he says is firmly supported by the words of Jesus as well as by the writings of the apostles.

But please don't imagine that what you're about to read is merely Marc's personal interpretation of Jesus' words. No what Marc presents can be corroborated by literally hundreds—if not thousands—of quotations from the early Christians who lived shortly after the apostles died. Marc's presentation may sound strange to some modern ears, but it would not have sounded the least bit strange to the men and women who personally heard the apostles teach and who could read the New Testament in their own native Greek. These were Christians who belonged to the churches the apostles founded, and many of them willingly died as martyrs for Christ and His gospel.

My prayer is that Marc's small book will arouse your interest and that, like the Bereans, you will search the Scriptures and the record of history to see if these things are really so.

David W. Bercot, editor of *A Dictionary of Early Christian Beliefs* and author of several books including *Will the Real Heretics Please Stand Up*, *The Kingdom that Turned the World Upside Down*, and *Will the Theologians Please Sit Down*.

Introduction

Openly discussing alternative views to the Gospel can be quite controversial. This is primarily because, among Protestants, there is near unanimity in the West as to how one is to be saved. Martin Luther and the reformers of the 16th century set off a chain of events that ultimately resulted in establishing a brand of Christianity that is all pervasive. Even sects that do not officially claim to trace a lineage to the reformers as their theological descendants unintentionally still borrow much of their doctrine from them. However, this begs the question: what if the reformers were mistaken?

We all know that the victors rewrite history. Well, this is especially true in church history. However, as with all history, the truth is readily available to those willing to look for it and open-minded enough to receive it.

We can trace our doctrinal beliefs to single individuals in history. Now I know that most of you, like I once did, assume that Luther and the reformers took their theology all the way back to the Apostles strictly based on the Scriptures. However, it doesn't take long to figure out that this is just one of the examples of revisionist church history that I just spoke about. As we discuss what one must do to be saved, you will more clearly understand exactly what I mean.

Problem...and Solution

In the beginning God created all things (Genesis 1). The culmination of His creation was humanity, created in His image (Genesis 1:26-27). In the Garden of Eden, the perfect place prepared for Adam and Eve, our first ancestors were deceived by Satan to disobey God, introducing the first sin to humanity. As a result, corruption entered Creation and the human race (Romans 5:19). In accordance with God's decree (that is the Law of Sin and Death— see Genesis 2:16, Romans 6:16, 8:2, and 8:13), Adam and Eve were ousted from the Garden and lost access to eternal life (Genesis 3:23-24). So from that day forth, the corruption introduced to humanity through our ancestral parents has given all humans a predisposition to sin. As Paul said: "for all have sinned and fall short of the glory of God," and Isaiah the prophet: "All of us like sheep have gone astray, Each of us has turned to his own way." Therefore, having alienated ourselves from God, we have become slaves to the one we obey (that is Satan), and through the Law of Sin and Death our end is shared with Satan and the other angels that rebelled against God. We await certain judgment and the Lake of Fire (see Romans 6:16 and Matthew 25:41). Satan laid claim on all men according to the Law of Sin and Death, and we were in bondage to him.

But God made a way. God sent His eternal Son Jesus: in nature, fully deity, one with the Father in likeness, but distinct in personhood. Jesus is the only begotten of the Father, true light shining from His Father's being, born of a virgin, taking the form of sinful man, yet without sin. Jesus was sent not to change His Father's mind about man, but rather change man's mind about the Father. Jesus, God incarnate, made His dwelling among men to show man how to live in accordance with the Father's will. Jesus, in the form of a man, humbly subjected Himself to all His Father's teachings and obeyed the Father to the fullest—even unto death on a cross (Philippians 2:8). Jesus taught the very words of the Father to all men and showed us how to live by His example, so that we would learn to walk as He did. His mission was to introduce us to God and His ways, so that we could turn our hearts back to the Father through Him.

Through Him, yes—because apart from Him, there is no freedom from sin. God, through His incredible mercy and grace, sent His only begotten Son, not just to turn our hearts to Himself, but also to destroy the devil's work, that is to set us free from the bondage of Sin and Death, and enslave us rather to righteousness.

God gave His Son into the hands of sinful men, who mocked Him, scourged Him, and nailed Him to a cross unto death. Jesus' blood flowed freely; it is by His blood our sins are cleansed, and by His broken body we are made whole.

We, being in bondage to Satan via the Law of Sin and Death, needed our freedom purchased. God offered His very own Son, perfect, without sin, in very nature deity in every way, yet in human likeness, as a ransom to purchase our freedom from Sin and Death (Hebrews 2:14-15). Jesus, because He was without sin, was not subject to the Law of Sin and Death. As a result, Death could not hold Him (Acts 2:24). Jesus plundered Hades, the underworld or abode of the dead, and preached the Gospel to the dead for three days. Having set the captives free, Jesus returned to the earth in bodily form, with the keys to Death and Hades in His hands (Revelation 1:18). In resurrected form, Jesus taught the disciples for 40 days concerning the Kingdom until His ascension to heaven, where He now rules His Kingdom at the right hand of the Father, in all His glory and splendor (Acts 1:3, 9, Hebrews 1:3, 12:2).

The Bible says that Christ was sent as a ransom (Matthew 20:28, 1 Timothy 2:6). Let us consider for a second the dynamic of a ransom scenario, which was all too common in biblical times. Who is the ransom normally paid to? The captor of course! So under the widely-accepted modern doctrine of the atonement, who is the ransom paid to? God the Father. Let me clarify. The satisfaction theory of atonement says that Jesus was sent by God to satisfy His own need for justice. Otherwise, the payer is also the payee.

Compare this to what the early church believed: man was taken into bondage by Satan, and held under the Law of Sin and Death. Jesus was sent by God to pay the ransom and free us. Makes sense, doesn't it? If you have read or watched *The Lion, the Witch and the Wardrobe* (Chronicles of Narnia) by C. S. Lewis, you have already been exposed to what once was the orthodox teaching of the atonement. The White Witch was Satan, Aslan was Jesus, Edmund was man, and the Deep Magic was the Law of Sin and Death. Edmund sinned and the Witch had a rightful claim to him because of the Deep Magic. Aslan was given as a ransom to free Edmund. Yet death could not hold Him because Aslan was innocent. This is how the deal went down for real.

Just like the white witch in Narnia overextended herself, in the real world Satan tried to grasp more than he was entitled to. He was allowed to abuse and torture Jesus. He was allowed to cruelly put Jesus to death on the cross. But he wanted to be able to hold

Jesus forever in Hades—something to which he had no legal right. In the end, Satan was outwitted because of his own evil. The Father resurrected Christ from the grave. Through Christ the Victor, we have a hero who voluntarily sacrificed Himself as a sheep for the slaughter, knowing that through it all, Death could not hold Him and He would plunder Hades and conquer Death. He gave His life as a ransom, suffering humiliation and great agony, in order to steal the keys of Death and Hades so that through Him, all who call upon Him would be saved from Sin, Death and Judgment. Through the ransom He paid, Christ has set men free from the Law of Sin and Death.

Through the incarnation of Christ the Teacher, the living Word, we have been introduced to the very will of God in Christ's life and teaching, such that we can simply repent and turn to Him and His ways. Our unconditional surrender, a broken and contrite heart, opens the floodgates of God's mercy. Through our baptism, we partake in Jesus' death and resurrection (Romans 6:1-7). The doors of Death and Hades are opened wide and we go through unscathed, our sins washed by the water and the cleansing blood of Christ. We come up from the waters, chains loosed, free to fellowship with God in all holiness and righteousness. The old man dies with Christ and the new man is birthed; we are born again and indwelled by the Holy Spirit, in the likeness of Christ's resurrection. The culmination of this mystery is our own bodily resurrection at the sounding of the last trumpet (1 Corinthians 15:51-52).

Now the purpose of the atonement is this: to restore our hearts back to God in true repentance, turning away from sin and towards holiness and righteousness. Our salvation is as sure as our changed heart. We are adopted as sons, grafted in as wild olive branches to the holy Vine, in communion with God and the saints—all partakers in the body and blood of Christ (John 6:54). Our invitation to the Vine comes by grace through faith, in repentance and baptism. We remain on the Vine by abiding in Christ. Abiding in Christ is maintaining our obedient love relationship with Him (see John 15:10 below and John 14:15 and 21). There can be some level of obedience without love, but there is no love without obedience. And without such fruit, the branches will be cut off and thrown into the fire (John 15:6 and Matthew 7:19). Our continued relationship with Christ, evidenced in our fruitfulness (that is, our obedient love relationship with Christ) demonstrates our perseverance in the faith and our hope for salvation (Luke 8:15).

Let us read the fifteenth chapter of John's gospel to see how Jesus says it:

> "I am the true vine, and My Father is the vinedresser. Every branch in Me that does not bear fruit, He takes away; and every branch that bears fruit, He prunes it so that it may bear more fruit. You are already clean because of the word which I have spoken to you. Abide in Me, and I in you. As the branch cannot bear fruit of itself unless it abides in the vine, so neither can you unless you abide in Me. I am the vine, you are the branches; he who abides in Me and I in him, he bears much fruit, for apart from Me you can do nothing. If anyone does not abide in Me, he is thrown away as a branch and dries up; and they gather them, and cast them into the fire and they are burned. If you abide in Me, and My words abide in you, ask whatever you wish, and it will be done for you. My Father is glorified by this, that you bear much fruit, and so prove to be My disciples. Just as the Father has loved Me, I have also loved you; abide in My love. If you keep My commandments, you will abide in My love; just as I have kept My Father's commandments and abide in His love. These things I have spoken to you so that My joy may be in you, and that your joy may be made full." (John 15:1-11)

It is clear in this passage that we are to both get on the Vine and remain on the Vine. We will revisit this passage later.

Thus far we briefly discussed several elements concerning the subject of salvation: man's fall, Christ's atonement, and the two discreet aspects of the Vine: getting on and remaining on. Next we will discuss the right foundation and related topics.

The Right Foundation

In chapter seven of Matthew's gospel, Jesus explicitly tells us that we must build on the rock. This is defined as hearing His words and obeying them. Those who hear His words and do not obey them build on sand, and will have a great fall. In the words of Christ:

> "Therefore everyone who hears these words of Mine and acts on them, may be compared to a wise man who built his house on the rock. And the rain fell, and the floods came, and the winds blew and slammed against that house; and yet it did not fall, for it had been founded on the rock. Everyone who hears these words of Mine and does not act on them, will be like a foolish man who built his house on the sand. The rain fell, and the floods came, and the winds blew and slammed against that house; and it fell—and great was its fall." (Matthew 7:24-27)

In context, "these words of Mine" refers to His teachings in the entire Sermon on the Mount. Interestingly, the first complete Christian apology (proof), composed by Justin Martyr and written to the Roman Emperor, Antoninus Pius, emphasizes these teachings. After detailing many of the specific teachings of Christ in his First Apology, Justin says this:

> And let those who are not found living as He taught, be understood to be no Christians, even though they profess with the lip the precepts of Christ; for not those who make profession, but those who do the works, shall be saved, according to His word: "Not every one who saith to Me, Lord, Lord, shall enter into the kingdom of heaven, but he that doeth the will of My Father which is in heaven. For whosoever heareth Me, and doeth My sayings, heareth Him that sent Me. And many will say unto Me, Lord, Lord, have we not eaten and drunk in Thy name, and done wonders? And then will I say unto them, Depart from Me, ye workers of iniquity. Then shall there be wailing and gnashing of teeth, when the righteous shall shine as the sun, and the wicked are sent into everlasting fire. For many shall come in My name, clothed outwardly in sheep's clothing, but inwardly being ravening wolves. By their works ye shall know them. And every tree that bringeth not forth good fruit, is hewn down and cast into

the fire." And as to those who are not living pursuant to these His teachings, and are Christians only in name, we demand that all such be punished by you.

Justin's understanding of these teachings is not unique to him. There is little doubt upon reading their writings that the early church unanimously understood Jesus' teachings to be supremely authoritative and to be taken quite literally.

Unfortunately, a modern understanding of the Gospel almost presupposes the need for a careful exegesis of Paul's letter to the Romans. However, this relegates the actual teachings and example of Christ to a secondary position. Yet Jesus Himself said no student is greater than His master (John 13:16 and 15:20). Interestedly, Jesus' first two commands (proclaimed throughout the Gospels) clearly articulate the early church view of the Gospel; that is, repent and follow me! The Gospel according to Jesus is turn from your sins and follow Him. Turn from the world, the kingdom of darkness, sin, selfishness, hatred, and submit to the lordship of Christ, the Kingdom of God, righteousness, holiness, obedience, and love. This is the true Gospel. Christ's atonement (that is, His incarnation, suffering, death, and resurrection) were accomplished to facilitate this specific end.

God did not simply send Jesus to suffer and die so as to satisfy His own justice. Christ was not merely a substitute for our own just punishment for errant behavior, and He did not simply come to earth to take away the penalty of our sin. If this were true, why then did Jesus teach at all? Why did He show us how to live if the atonement was simply a legal transaction?

This "satisfaction" model of the atonement, though widely accepted by Protestants and Catholics alike, was not introduced until about 1100 AD by Anselm, the Catholic Archbishop of Canterbury. For 1100 years, this form of teaching was foreign—foreign to the Apostles, the early church, and everyone else. Yet, it is upon this foundation that the modern Gospel firmly rests. The result: a Gospel of "easy believism." Since the penal substitution or satisfaction theory of atonement cleanses those who believe through Christ's death on the cross, the work starts and finishes on the cross. Therefore, no repentance, no obedience, no holiness, no righteousness, no fruit, and no change of allegiance establishing Christ as Lord is deemed necessary in the one who professes to believe. The end is a "salvation" that does not require a heart turned to God. The result is a "gospel" quite at odds with the Gospel according to Jesus; "repent and follow me" is replaced with simply "believe in me." This is one of the greatest deceptions the enemy has ever introduced to humanity. Satan, as he did in the Garden, again says, "Hath God really said?"

A clear understanding of why God sent Jesus to earth—that is, the incarnation and atonement—will lead to a proper understanding of salvation and even eternal security. So let us continue to discuss these vital doctrines. But before we do, let us discuss God's nature with respect to humanity: just or merciful.

Justice or Mercy

God is merciful. Everyone would agree with that statement. However, the satisfaction (or penal substitution) theory of the atonement presents a God who actually is not merciful, because He is first and foremost just. Let me explain.

Anselm's theory of the atonement indicates that God has been wronged by sinful man (we would all agree with that part), and that God was so offended that restitution needs to be made to Him. Our sincere heartfelt remorse and earnest repentance are insufficient to turn His wrath away, because our offense is too great. We must face the punishment for our sins because God's justice demands it. However, since the offense was made by man, a man having committed no offense could take the penalty upon himself to pay the restitution, satisfying God's requirement for justice.

However, does this image of the Father show that He is merciful? According to this view, God is not willing to forgive our debt, but rather requires another to pay it instead. He technically shows no mercy at all, but rather just puts the wrath on another. The debt payment is still required in full. There is no forgiveness of the debt at all.

Worse yet, He actually sends His most beloved Son to suffer and die at His own hands, to satisfy His own demands for justice, because His very nature can't simply extend mercy and forgiveness. This justice actually makes Him a tyrant.

This atonement model also limits Christ's blood to a payment of sorts, clearing a ledger, making restitution for damages incurred by the Father. However, Scripture tells us that the blood of Christ actually cleanses us, washing away our sins—literally changing us (1 John 1:7), not just erasing the ledgers of heaven.

In contrast, the real God has always been merciful to those who humble themselves before Him in repentance—that is, turning away from sin and unto righteousness. Look at the people of Nineveh, or the Israelites numerous times in their history. God's offer for forgiveness of sins has always been open to all who come to him with a broken and contrite spirit, as the Psalmist states: "The sacrifices of God are a broken spirit; A broken and a contrite heart, O God, You will not despise" (Psalm 51:17). Forgiveness is available to all who come to Him. However, our predisposition to sin from the corruption through the lineage of Adam prevails in our flesh. Regardless of our desire to please God, we still fall short as a result of this bondage to sin (Romans 7:14-24). Breaking us free from the bondage of corruption is the true reason why the Father sent Christ to die at the hand of sinners. Christ came to destroy the devil's works (1 John 3:8).

Let us see how Jesus explained forgiveness in His parable in Matthew 18.

> Then Peter came and said to Him, "Lord, how often shall my brother sin against me and I forgive him? Up to seven times?" Jesus said to him, "I do not say to you, up to seven times, but up to seventy times seven. For this reason the kingdom of heaven may be compared to a king who wished to settle accounts with his slaves. When he had begun to settle them, one who owed him ten thousand talents was brought to him. But since he did not have the means to repay, his lord commanded him to be sold, along with his wife and children and all that he had, and repayment to be made. So the slave fell to the ground and prostrated himself before him, saying, 'Have patience with me and I will repay you everything.' And the lord of that slave felt compassion and released him and forgave him the debt. But that slave went out and found one of his fellow slaves who owed him a hundred denarii; and he seized him and began to choke him, saying, 'Pay back what you owe.' So his fellow slave fell to the ground and began to plead with him, saying, 'Have patience with me and I will repay you.' But he was unwilling and went and threw him in prison until he should pay back what was owed. So when his fellow slaves saw what had happened, they were deeply grieved and came and reported to their lord all that had happened. Then summoning him, his lord said to him, 'You wicked slave, I forgave you all that debt because you pleaded with me. Should you not also have had mercy on your fellow slave, in the same way that I had mercy on you?' And his lord, moved with anger, handed him over to the torturers until he should repay all that was owed him. My heavenly Father will also do the same to you, if each of you does not forgive his brother from your heart." (Matthew 18:21-35)

Peter asked Jesus how many times he should forgive someone. In response, Jesus told him a story about a king (the Father) settling accounts with his slaves (men). A slave owed a debt he could not pay and the king demanded payment. However, the slave pled for mercy, and the king was moved with compassion. Here is when, according to Anselm's theory of the atonement, a man with no debt would step in and pay the balance of the account, because the king's requirement for justice necessitated payment in full. But this does not happen. Instead, the king simply released him and forgave the debt. This is a picture of God's mercy.

There's another important point. We also see here that the forgiveness of the slave's debt was conditional. When the slave refused to forgive his debtor, the king, in turn, held him accountable for his previously forgiven personal debts. If Anselm's theory were true, this could not be. If Jesus supposedly erased the ledger by His payment for our sins, payment was made, and God could never hold us accountable for that debt again. However, if our debt is forgiven simply by God's mercy (based on sincere remorse and repentance), God can justly reinstate the sin to our account if we fail to manifest that repentance and live it out with our fellow man. And Jesus clearly states in this passage (as He did in the Lord's prayer) that if we fail to forgive our debtors, we will not be forgiven.

Lastly, does God really expect more from us than He was willing to do Himself? The point of this entire story was to answer Peter's question concerning man forgiving man. Jesus illustrates that we must forgive as God did. But with Anselm's theory, God demanded justice and full payment. If this were true, it would be consistent and appropriate for us to demand the same. Clearly this does not reconcile with the Gospel.

In the next chapter, I will introduce a subject that is all but lost in today's churches, though it is the very theme of Jesus' teachings—the Kingdom of God.

The Kingdom of God

Jesus ushered in the Kingdom of God. In fact, He mentions the Kingdom over 100 times in the four Gospels. The Kingdom of God is the theme of a great many of His parables. In fact, the Gospel is called "the Gospel of the Kingdom" several times. Yet today, the gospel that is preached concerns only Jesus' substitutionary death for our sins—rarely about His Kingdom. As a result, many evangelicals don't even know what the Kingdom of God is.

Some assume that the Kingdom of God will not manifest itself until Christ's second coming. This is understandable, since some passages are clearly a reference to the culmination of Kingdom when Christ reigns here on earth. However, Jesus likewise taught plainly that the Kingdom of God was ushered in at the time of His public ministry, with statements such as, "the Kingdom of God is at hand." Some also assume that for the present at least, the Kingdom of God is simply a spiritual kingdom. In actuality, it is a *real* kingdom—here on earth, yes, even now. Let me explain.

What makes up a kingdom? All kingdoms have four elements: a king, a domain, laws, and citizenry. Well, so does the Kingdom of God. Jesus is the king. The domain is heaven and earth. The laws are the commands of Christ. The citizenry are those who "subject" themselves to the king. Now it is apparent that the Kingdom of God certainly differs from earthly kingdoms quite a bit. First of all, our king currently reigns from His throne in heaven. Most kings preside over their kingdoms among their subjects. However, Jesus made it clear that the domain is both heaven and earth (Matthew 6:10 and 28:18). This is just another example of the reason for the incarnation, so that the king would walk among His subjects. The second coming will usher in a period of the king reigning with His subjects here on earth. Therein lies why some presume that the Kingdom of God does not actually begin until His second coming. However, He reigns now, even if He resides in heaven.

So then we come to the laws. Jesus came with many teachings. Many think they are optional. However, I already discussed that to remain on the Vine we must abide in Christ; that is, obeying the King's commands. I likewise discussed that building on the rock means obeying His commands. Let me provide a third illustration also from the Sermon on the Mount. Jesus taught:

> "Not everyone who says to Me, 'Lord, Lord,' will enter the kingdom of heaven, but he who does the will of My Father

who is in heaven will enter. "Many will say to Me on that day, 'Lord, Lord, did we not prophesy in Your name, and in Your name cast out demons, and in Your name perform many miracles?' "And then I will declare to them, 'I never knew you; DEPART FROM ME, YOU WHO PRACTICE LAWLESSNESS.'" (Matthew 7:21-23)

Here Jesus explains how we enter the Kingdom, specifically referencing the culmination of the Kingdom as I mentioned earlier. The term used here is the "kingdom of heaven." Careful study shows us that the Kingdom of God and Kingdom of heaven are synonymous, with preference given by certain gospel writers to one term versus the other. This is apparent by reading parallel passages in various gospel accounts and seeing the same exact story given with variant use of the two terms (compare Matthew 13 to Mark 4, for example).

It is clear that this passage refers to judgment (note the reference to "that day"), and is clearly discussing salvation. However, my point here is exclusively the treatment of the subject of the Kingdom laws. Jesus makes it obvious that selection on judgment day is based not simply on believing, but doing the will of His Father. Jesus also does not regard signs and wonders as pertinent to salvation, but rather He chastises those who merely call Him Lord, as "you who practice lawlessness." Clear from this passage is the fact that there are indeed LAWS; for if rejection is for practicing lawlessness, then there are certainly laws given.

So what are these laws? Pauline writings (specifically Romans and Galatians) make it clear that one can not be saved through following the Law of Moses: circumcision, adherence to days, months, seasons and years, specific diet, and so on. The council in Jerusalem further clarifies that the only burdens from the Jewish teachings that apply to the Gentiles were abstaining from fornication, abstaining from things sacrificed to idols, and not eating blood and strangled animals (Acts 15:28-29). No regard is given to the Mosaic Law here. So we can confidently conclude that it is not the Law of Moses that Jesus is referring to (see also Hebrews 8:7-13)

However, Jesus did say that unless our righteousness surpasses that of the religious leaders of His day, we would not enter the Kingdom of heaven (Matthew 5:20). But Jesus then clearly teaches what He means. He goes through precepts from the Mosaic Law, one item at a time, and explains what His expectations are by stating, "You have heard it said [in the Law], *but I say*..." If you read His teaching, you will see that He raises the bar big time! He does not take away the Law, but expands on it and clarifies His expectations. It is following this dissertation that Jesus shares what "lawlessness" is, explaining that those who hear "these words of mine" and act upon them build on the rock and those who neglect them build on sand, resulting is certain destruction. But that begs the question: what about the rest of the Old Testament teachings that Jesus does not explicitly address in His teachings?

Jesus says that He did not come to abolish the Law, but rather fulfill it. He then says that not the least letter will be taken away until it is "accomplished." This meaning the fulfillment of the messianic prophesies and His work on earth (see Luke 18:31, John 19:28-30, John 17:4, and Matthew 26:56).

We read in John's gospel of Jesus telling the Jews, "You search the Scriptures because you think that in them you have eternal life; it is these that testify about Me; and you are unwilling to come to Me that you might have life" (John 5:39-40). When Jesus says "the Scriptures," He is specifically referencing what we today refer to as the Old Testament. He makes it clear that eternal life is through Him, not the Old Testament teachings. Jesus further elaborates during the Upper Room discourse with His disciples on the night He was betrayed, "If you keep My commandments, you will abide in My love; just as I have kept My Father's commandments and abide in His love." (John 15:10). Here Jesus makes it clear that He submitted to His Father and obeyed all His commandments, abiding in His love. Jesus, in this passage says He fulfilled the Law by obeying all of His Father's commands (in turn fulfilling all the prophesy); now in the same way as Jesus obeyed His Father's commands, we are to obey Jesus' commands. The baton has been passed to us. For Jesus' teachings are precisely what the Father commanded Him to say, and even Moses directed all to listen to Him (see Deuteronomy 18:15-19, John 7:16-17, and John 12:44-50)

Another clear example from Jesus concerning our requirement to observe His commands is the Great Commission passage in Matthew's gospel. Jesus says to His disciples:

And Jesus came up and spoke to them, saying, "All authority has been given to Me in heaven and on earth. Go therefore and make disciples of all the nations, baptizing them in the name of the Father and the Son and the Holy Spirit, teaching them to observe all that I commanded you; and lo, I am with you always, even to the end of the age." (Matthew 28:18-20)

Here Jesus commands His disciples to make more disciples, teaching them to observe all that He commanded them. This clear instruction is obviously meant to carry forth through the ages, as each successive generation of disciples is explicitly commanded to both observe this command and teach the next generation to observe ALL His commands. Jesus did not leave us guessing what the new "law" is: it is His commands! Therefore our faith must be derived from the *red letters* (see also John 14:21, 23-24, Hebrews 8:7-13,).

So that leaves us with the final aspect of the Kingdom: citizenry. Again, Jesus does not leave us guessing. He speaks quite a bit on the matter. In fact, we have already discussed several pertinent teachings.

Citizens of the Kingdom

There are two aspects to citizenry in the Kingdom: gaining citizenship, and keeping citizenship. This may be foreign to some, but we will look at the Scriptures to clarify this concept. Jesus' teaching on the Vine and the branches in the fifteenth chapter of John's gospel reveals that the branches were on the Vine. They are clean because of Jesus' words. Yet, we also see that the branches will be cut off and thrown into the fire if they do not bear fruit—later defined by loving obedience (see verses 6 and 10). Therefore, two aspects are present: getting on the vine and staying on the vine—what I've referred to as gaining citizenship and keeping citizenship.

Jesus says again in the Sermon on the Mount: "Every tree that does not bear good fruit is cut down and thrown into the fire" (Matthew 7:19). John the Baptist put it this way, chastising the religious Jews who presumed their salvation was assured in spite of their refusal to repent:

> "Therefore bear fruit in keeping with repentance; and do not suppose that you can say to yourselves, 'We have Abraham for our father'; for I say to you that from these stones God is able to raise up children to Abraham. The axe is already laid at the root of the trees; therefore every tree that does not bear good fruit is cut down and thrown into the fire." (Matthew 3:8-10)

Jesus taught similarly about repentance following the terrible deaths and disgrace of some Israelites:

> "I tell you, no, but unless you repent, you will all likewise perish." And He began telling this parable: "A man had a fig tree which had been planted in his vineyard; and he came looking for fruit on it and did not find any. And he said to the vineyard-keeper, 'Behold, for three years I have come looking for fruit on this fig tree without finding any. Cut it down! Why does it even use up the ground?' "And he answered and said to him, 'Let it alone, sir, for this year too, until I dig around it and put in fertilizer; and if it bears fruit next year, fine; but if not, cut it down.'" (Luke 13:5-9)

So we see that repentance is absolutely necessary for entrance into the Kingdom. Yet it does not stop there. Jesus is specific that entrance isn't enough. We must *keep* our citizenship.

Here are a couple parables concerning the Kingdom.

> Jesus presented another parable to them, saying, "The kingdom of heaven may be compared to a man who sowed good seed in his field. But while his men were sleeping, his enemy came and sowed tares among the wheat, and went away. But when the wheat sprouted and bore grain, then the tares became evident also. The slaves of the landowner came and said to him, 'Sir, did you not sow good seed in your field? How then does it have tares?' And he said to them, 'An enemy has done this!' The slaves said to him, 'Do you want us, then, to go and gather them up?' But he said, 'No; for while you are gathering up the tares, you may uproot the wheat with them. 'Allow both to grow together until the harvest; and in the time of the harvest I will say to the reapers, First gather up the tares and bind them in bundles to burn them up; but gather the wheat into my barn.'"…
>
> Then He left the crowds and went into the house And His disciples came to Him and said, "Explain to us the parable of the tares of the field." And He said, "The one who sows the good seed is the Son of Man, and the field is the world; and as for the good seed, these are the sons of the kingdom; and the tares are the sons of the evil one; and the enemy who sowed them is the devil, and the harvest is the end of the age; and the reapers are angels. So just as the tares are gathered up and burned with fire, so shall it be at the end of the age. The Son of Man will send forth His angels, and they will gather out of His kingdom all stumbling blocks, and those who commit lawlessness, and will throw them into the furnace of fire; in that place there will be weeping and gnashing of teeth. Then THE RIGHTEOUS WILL SHINE FORTH AS THE SUN in the kingdom of their Father He who has ears, let him hear." (Matthew 13:24-30, 36-43)

In this parable, we see that the Kingdom of God contains both good and evil; those who practice lawlessness are thrown in the fire, and the righteous will go to be with the Father. Some interpret this passage as meaning that the sons of the kingdom are the churched and the sons of the evil one are the unchurched or the unbelievers of the world. However, the parable teaches that the wheat was planted before the tares and the tares were introduced among the wheat after the wheat was planted. Clearly, the church was planted and then apostasy was introduced into the church. The early church understood this parable to mean that the church would be polluted by stumbling blocks and those who commit lawlessness. In light of the next parable, the parable of the dragnet (taught by Jesus in the same sermon as the parable of the wheat and tares) it will become obvious why this was a logical conclusion.

> "Again, the kingdom of heaven is like a dragnet cast into the sea, and gathering fish of every kind; and when it was filled, they drew it up on the beach; and they sat down and gathered the good fish into containers, but the bad they threw away. So it will be at the end of the age; the angels will come forth and take out the wicked from among the righteous, and will throw them into the furnace of fire; in that place there will be weeping and gnashing of teeth." (Matthew 13:47-50)

There is little ambiguity here that the Kingdom of God [heaven] IS the dragnet. And clearly, the net will capture both good and bad fish. The fish will then be sorted at the end of the age. Comparing the dragnet to the wheat and tares, it is easy to see why the tares were interpreted as being an apostate part of the church. We will see in the next chapter more on the subject of "good and bad" citizens of the Kingdom.

Dress Code

The parables of the wheat and tares and the dragnet are not the only ones that discuss the second aspect of citizenship—that is, keeping it or remaining on the Vine. Here is the parable of the wedding feast.

"The kingdom of heaven may be compared to a king who gave a wedding feast for his son. And he sent out his slaves to call those who had been invited to the wedding feast, and they were unwilling to come. Again he sent out other slaves saying, 'Tell those who have been invited, "Behold, I have prepared my dinner; my oxen and my fattened livestock are all butchered and everything is ready; come to the wedding feast."' But they paid no attention and went their way, one to his own farm, another to his business, and the rest seized his slaves and mistreated them and killed them. But the king was enraged, and he sent his armies and destroyed those murderers and set their city on fire. Then he said to his slaves, 'The wedding is ready, but those who were invited were not worthy. 'Go therefore to the main highways, and as many as you find there, invite to the wedding feast.' Those slaves went out into the streets and gathered together all they found, both evil and good; and the wedding hall was filled with dinner guests. But when the king came in to look over the dinner guests, he saw a man there who was not dressed in wedding clothes, and he said to him, 'Friend, how did you come in here without wedding clothes?' And the man was speechless. Then the king said to the servants, 'Bind him hand and foot, and throw him into the outer darkness; in that place there will be weeping and gnashing of teeth.' For many are called, but few are chosen." (Matthew 22:2-14)

This passage illustrates three groups of people: the Jews who rejected the invitation and treated the messengers shamefully. They never made it to the wedding (into the Kingdom). Then we have the mass invitation (or "dragnet") of both good and evil. The parable ends with singling out the dinner guest who did not have wedding clothes. The passage itself does not define what is meant by the wedding clothes; however, Scripture is not silent on the subject. In Jesus' discourse to the church in Sardis, He says this:

'I know your deeds, that you have a name that you are alive, but you are dead. Wake up, and strengthen the things that remain, which were about to die; for I have not found your deeds completed in the sight of My God. So remember what you have received and heard; and keep it, and repent. Therefore if you do not wake up, I will come like a thief, and you will not know at what hour I will come to you. But you have a few people in Sardis who have not soiled their garments; and they will walk with Me in white, for they are worthy. He who overcomes will thus be clothed in white garments; and I will not erase his name from the book of life, and I will confess his name before My Father and before His angels.' (Revelation 3:1-5)

Here Jesus tells the church they have a name that they are alive, but are dead. Their deeds are incomplete, and as a result, their garments are soiled. If they do not repent, their names will be erased from the book of life. Only the worthy will walk with Him. So in this passage, we see people that have been grafted in to the Vine, but are at serious risk of being cut off (names erased from the book of life). They have gained their citizenship into the Kingdom of God, but may lose it without repentance.

Incomplete deeds results in soiled garments—Jesus' words are clear. The garments are even more clearly defined elsewhere, in the context of the actual marriage supper no less. Scripture always defines Scripture.

"Let us rejoice and be glad and give the glory to Him, for the marriage of the Lamb has come and His bride has made herself ready. It was given to her to clothe herself in fine linen, bright and clean; for the fine linen is the righteous acts of the saints." (Revelation 19:7-8)

Here we see that it was given to the bride (the church of Christ—that is, citizens of the Kingdom), to CLOTHE HERSELF. The bride has MADE HERSELF READY. Her citizenship, her grafting to the Vine is by God's grace through faith—a result of the atonement of Christ. Yet the atonement does not stop there. Her keeping her citizenship, or remaining on the Vine is done by her, "given to her" by God to do. And what is the fine linen? Yes indeed, the righteous acts of the saints.

So how does this compare to the passages that state that salvation is entirely a work of God? Well, let's read one of the most persuasive passages used to promote that position:

> For by grace you have been saved through faith; and that not of yourselves, it is the gift of God; not as a result of works, so that no one may boast. For we are His workmanship, created in Christ Jesus for good works, which God prepared beforehand so that we would walk in them. (Ephesians 2:8-10)

Well, we are indeed saved by grace through faith, because it was Christ who willfully subjected Himself to the Father, was given into the hands of evil men, bled and died so that He could conquer death and set us free from the Law of Sin and Death. It was His blood that washed us clean. Getting on the Vine is only through Him, for He IS the Vine!

However, let's not stop reading at verse 9. Verse 10 says we are His workmanship created in Christ to do good works. Our freedom from sin, the atonement of Christ, had an inherent objective. Remember the Gospel according to Jesus: repent and follow Him. We are to turn from evil and embrace good. We are to do what He saved us to do. And the Scriptures declare, if we fail to do so, we are at risk for losing our citizenship. Our citizenship in the Kingdom of God is dependent on our subjection to the King, and obedience to the King's laws—that is, the commands of Christ.

Filthy Rags?

But doesn't the Bible teach that our righteous acts are filthy rags? No, this is simply another example of a revisionist Christian history. Nothing could be more pleasing to God than our continued righteousness; it is for this reason God sent His Son, that we would be righteous and holy.

So where does the myth come from? It's based in reformed theology. According to this doctrine, man has literally zero role in his salvation. Further, man couldn't do good even if he wanted to. The reformers taught that we could not come to Christ by faith even if we wanted to, but rather it was entirely (and arbitrarily) predestined by God who would and who wouldn't come to Him. One of the natural conclusions of this theology is that even the good we do, is inherently evil. Isaiah 64:6 is used to support this theology; however, before the reformers, this verse was rarely, if ever, quoted by the early church—it was apparently considered of little consequence. Yet, as a result of the importance of this concept to the reformer's doctrine of total depravity, it is one of the most oft quoted passages of the Old Testament today. Here it is:

> But we are all as an unclean thing, and all our righteousnesses are as filthy rags; and we all do fade as a leaf; and our iniquities, like the wind, have taken us away. (Isaiah 64:6)

Now I encourage you to read it in context. This is Isaiah speaking in a penitent prayer to God, referencing and speaking on behalf of rebellious Israel. This is not God speaking about all of humanity for all time, but rather an emotional plea to God for a rebellious people, a very specific people—the prophet's contemporaries.

Simply do a biblical word search for "righteous," "upright," and even "blameless" to see what you come up with. Regardless of translation, you will find literally hundreds of references to men and women who were considered "righteous" before God apart from Christ—that is, without an "imputed righteousness." You will likewise find numerous references in the wisdom literature of the righteous commended by God. There is equal consistency in the New Testament. Prior to faith in Christ, Zacharias, Elizabeth, John the Baptist, Joseph the father of Jesus, Simeon, Joseph of Arimathea, and Cornelius were all called "righteous" and were praised for their conduct. This certainly does not mean these people were without sin (see for example Romans 3:9-10); it just means that they lived their lives pleasing to God, striving to adhere to His precepts. Never does God consider this filthy or bad.

In fact, John, the beloved apostle of Jesus' inner circle, said this in his first epistle:

> And everyone who has this hope fixed on Him purifies himself, just as He is pure. Everyone who practices sin also practices lawlessness; and sin is lawlessness. You know that He appeared in order to take away sins; and in Him there is no sin. No one who abides in Him sins; no one who sins has seen Him or knows Him. Little children, make sure no one deceives you; *the one who practices righteousness is righteous*, just as He is righteous; the one who practices sin is of the devil; for the devil has sinned from the beginning. The Son of God appeared for this purpose, to destroy the works of the devil. No one who is born of God practices sin, because His seed abides in him; and he cannot sin, because he is born of God. By this the children of God and the children of the devil are obvious: *anyone who does not practice righteousness is not of God*, nor the one who does not love his brother. (1 John 3:3-10, emphasis added)

In this single passage we see concurrence with what we have covered thus far. Lawlessness is defined here as sin, (that is, disobedience to Christ's law), consistent with the passages we discussed in Matthew 7 and 13. We also see that Jesus came to destroy the works of the devil; not just to forgive our sins, but rather to free us from sin—to break the chains and release us from the Law of Sin and Death. Again, His atonement was to change us, not just to perform a legal transaction.

However, the passage was here introduced to dispel the myth of imputed righteousness. Jesus did not suffer and die for us to simply accept a hypothetical, spiritual "righteousness" that in actuality never manifests itself in our lives. He came to destroy the works of the devil, so that through Him we would be reborn free from the bondage of sin, and walk in ACTUAL righteousness by the power of the Holy Spirit. John says that he who PRACTICES righteousness IS righteous, not he who simply believes himself to be righteous "in Christ." In fact, he explicitly says MAKE SURE NO ONE DECEIVES YOU otherwise! Have we accepted the deception of a false "gospel?" John again says that the one who does not practice righteousness is of the devil. This is no symbolic righteousness here; clearly one can not "practice" something that is not real. This refers to a genuine, lived-out righteousness, the purpose of Christ's atonement!

Don't Forget Part Two

The concept of a two-part salvation was unanimous among the early church. In fact, the only ones in early church history to believe in much of what is now considered orthodox—that is: total depravity, arbitrary predestination, and unconditional eternal security—were the Gnostics. That's right, the heretics John warned us about in his letters—the very ones the early church disputed for centuries—are the only people of the period who subscribed to these ideas. Why did the early church have unanimity on what moderns would consider heresy? It's because it is what Jesus and the Apostles taught!

We have already seen Jesus teach consistently concerning both aspects of salvation—described here as gaining citizenship in the Kingdom by grace through faith and then retaining citizenship though an obedient love relationship with Christ, abiding in Him. Paul provided a similar illustration in his letter to the church in Corinth through the witness of the Israelites:

> For I do not want you to be unaware, brethren, that our fathers were all under the cloud and all passed through the sea; and all were baptized into Moses in the cloud and in the sea; and all ate the same spiritual food; and all drank the same spiritual drink, for they were drinking from a spiritual rock which followed them; and the rock was Christ. Nevertheless, with most of them God was not well-pleased; for they were laid low in the wilderness. Now these things happened as examples for us, so that we would not crave evil things as they also craved. Do not be idolaters, as some of them were; as it is written, "THE PEOPLE SAT DOWN TO EAT AND DRINK, AND STOOD UP TO PLAY." Nor let us act immorally, as some of them did, and twenty-three thousand fell in one day. Nor let us try the Lord, as some of them did, and were destroyed by the serpents. Nor grumble, as some of them did, and were destroyed by the destroyer. Now these things happened to them as an example, and they were written for our instruction, upon whom the ends of the ages have come. Therefore let him who thinks he stands take heed that he does not fall. (1 Corinthians 10:1-12)

Jude, the brother of our Lord, in the fifth verse of his letter says likewise: "Now I desire to remind you, though you know all things once for all, that the Lord, after saving a people out of the land of Egypt, subsequently destroyed those who did not believe" (Jude verse 5).

Most of us are familiar with the story of the Exodus from Egypt. God displayed signs and wonders to ultimately cause the Pharaoh of Egypt to release their Jewish slaves. The culmination of the miracles was the saving of all the Israelite first born through the blood of the unblemished passover lamb.

Through God's miraculous intervention, the Israelites were saved from the land of Egypt, over 600,000 men of fighting age and an unspecified number of woman and children. This puts a total count of 2 million conservatively. The Israelites are saved from their Egyptian bondage by walking on dry land through the Red Sea. This is an incredible demonstration of God's grace and His power to save.

But that is not the end of the story—though we moderns often stop there. An important point to consider is: how many people actually made it to the promised land? Just TWO! The freed Israelites proved to be disobedient, obstinate, idolatrous, grumblers, and even cowards, all due to their unbelief. The result? Even though they were saved out of Egypt, simply two men of fighting age ever made it to the promised land. The reason? Paul's letter to the Hebrews says sin and disobedience, from unbelief:

> For who provoked Him when they had heard? Indeed, did not all those who came out of Egypt led by Moses? And with whom was He angry for forty years? Was it not with *those who sinned*, whose bodies fell in the wilderness? And to whom did He swear that they would not enter His rest, but to *those who were disobedient*? So we see that they were not able to enter because of unbelief. Therefore, let us fear if, while a promise remains of entering His rest, any one of you may seem to have come short of it. (Hebrews 3:16-4:1, emphasis added)

Well, Paul and Jude explain that this event occurred for our example. Clearly, the passover lamb was a type of Christ's voluntary sacrifice and shed blood. Walking through the Red Sea symbolizes baptism. Being saved from Egypt is symbolic of being saved from our bondage to Sin and Death, Egypt representing the fallen world. The desert represents our time of testing and growth—our opportunity to demonstrate our faith through obedience, surrender, and spiritual purity. The promised land represents heaven, which comes through struggle and perseverance, requiring courage and commitment.

Now looking at the account of the Exodus and comparing it to our Christian experience, we see that the shed blood of Christ, baptism, and being saved from Sin and Death do NOT guarantee entrance to heaven. It takes perseverance in the faith and obedience to get to the pearly gates; it takes an honest following of Jesus. Yet when most people use the word "saved," it means saved *into* heaven. On the other hand, when the New Testament authors say someone is "saved," they mean saved from Sin and Death—free to walk in holiness and righteousness. Eternal life will only be obtained through actually walking in holiness and righteousness.

Paul said in his letter to the Romans: "But now having been freed from sin and enslaved to God, you derive your benefit, resulting in sanctification, and the outcome, eternal life" (Romans 6:22). I urge you to read the entire chapter on your own for context. However for brevity, let's focus on this single passage. Here we see that through Christ we are freed from sin and enslaved to God. This in turn results in our sanctification (or holiness). The outcome: eternal life. Being saved from the Law of Sin and Death sets us free from sin, enabling us to be holy. It is this holiness "in the desert of life" that makes us worthy to walk with Christ in white (remember Revelation chapter 3).

So does that mean that we have no eternal security? Well, yes and no.

Secure in Christ

Remember earlier I said that our eternal security is only as certain as our turning to God. Following Christ is a sure way to get to heaven, for that is where He is! But if we for a second think we can follow after our flesh, sin, and the world and end up at the pearly gates, we are seriously deceived.

Paul said in the letter to the Hebrews (in my opinion, the single most sobering passage in Scripture).

> For if we go on sinning willfully after receiving the knowledge of the truth, there no longer remains a sacrifice for sins, but a terrifying expectation of judgment and THE FURY OF A FIRE WHICH WILL CONSUME THE ADVERSARIES. Anyone who has set aside the Law of Moses dies without mercy on the testimony of two or three witnesses. How much severer punishment do you think he will deserve who has trampled under foot the Son of God, and has regarded as unclean the blood of the covenant by which he was sanctified, and has insulted the Spirit of grace? For we know Him who said, "VENGEANCE IS MINE, I WILL REPAY " And again, "THE LORD WILL JUDGE HIS PEOPLE." It is a terrifying thing to fall into the hands of the living God. (Hebrews 10:26-31)

Therefore, willful sinning after turning to God gives us plenty of confidence that we await a "terrifying expectation of judgment." The doctrine of *unconditional* eternal security was foreign to the New Testament writers and the early church.

However, Scripture does speak of *conditional* eternal security. In John's first epistle, he states: "These things I have written to you who believe in the name of the Son of God, so that you may know that you have eternal life." (1 John 5:13). "These things" refers to the actual contents of the letter. Interestingly, a condensed version of this verse is used in a very popular evangelism program to prove that we can be confident in **un-**conditional eternal security, with absolutely no reference to the contents of the letter itself. This is very deceptive.

So what were the "things" John wrote that would assure us we have eternal life? Here are some excerpts from the letter. Notice the *conditional* ("if/then") statements:

If we say that we have fellowship with Him and yet walk in the darkness, we lie and do not practice the truth; but if we walk in the Light as He Himself is in the Light, we have fellowship with one another, and the blood of Jesus His Son cleanses us from all sin. (1 John 1:6-7)

By this we know that we have come to know Him, if we keep His commandments. The one who says, "I have come to know Him," and does not keep His commandments, is a liar, and the truth is not in him; but whoever keeps His word, in him the love of God has truly been perfected. By this we know that we are in Him: the one who says he abides in Him ought himself to walk in the same manner as He walk. (1 John 2:3-6)

Do not love the world nor the things in the world. If anyone loves the world, the love of the Father is not in him. For all that is in the world, the lust of the flesh and the lust of the eyes and the boastful pride of life, is not from the Father, but is from the world. The world is passing away, and also its lusts; but the one who does the will of God lives forever. (1 John 2:15-17)

Everyone who practices sin also practices lawlessness; and sin is lawlessness. You know that He appeared in order to take away sins; and in Him there is no sin. No one who abides in Him sins; no one who sins has seen Him or knows Him. Little children, make sure no one deceives you; the one who practices righteousness is righteous, just as He is righteous; the one who practices sin is of the devil; for the devil has sinned from the beginning. The Son of God appeared for this purpose, to destroy the works of the devil. No one who is born of God practices sin, because His seed abides in him; and he cannot sin, because he is born of God. By this the children of God and the children of the devil are obvious: anyone who does not practice righteousness is not of God, nor the one who does not love his brother. (1 John 3:4-10)

So what are some of the conditions John covered "that we might know we have eternal life?"

- Walk in the light, not darkness
- Keep Jesus' commandments
- Walk as Jesus walked

- Do not love the world or anything in the world
- Do the will of the Father
- Abide in Christ
- Practice righteousness
- And cease from sin

Did anyone go through this list with you when the "gospel" was presented to you?

Careful scrutiny reveals that this is simply the Gospel according to Jesus all over again; that is: repent and follow Him! Therefore, the only *condition* for eternal security is repenting and following Jesus. It's really that simple. Unfortunately it has been replaced by "believe in Him."

Count the Cost

So what did Jesus teach concerning following Him? In the fourteenth chapter of Luke's gospel account, Jesus told a large crowd of prospective followers what it would take to become His disciples. He certainly was not emulating the attractional, ear-tickling models of the modern church:

> Now large crowds were going along with Him; and He turned and said to them, "If anyone comes to Me, and does not hate his own father and mother and wife and children and brothers and sisters, yes, and even his own life, he cannot be My disciple. Whoever does not carry his own cross and come after Me cannot be My disciple. For which one of you, when he wants to build a tower, does not first sit down and calculate the cost to see if he has enough to complete it? Otherwise, when he has laid a foundation and is not able to finish, all who observe it begin to ridicule him, saying, 'This man began to build and was not able to finish.' Or what king, when he sets out to meet another king in battle, will not first sit down and consider whether he is strong enough with ten thousand men to encounter the one coming against him with twenty thousand? Or else, while the other is still far away, he sends a delegation and asks for terms of peace. So then, none of you can be My disciple who does not give up all his own possessions. Therefore, salt is good; but if even salt has become tasteless, with what will it be seasoned? It is useless either for the soil or for the manure pile; it is thrown out. He who has ears to hear, let him hear." (Luke 14:25-35)

There is a lot here. First of all, Jesus commands total allegiance. Nothing is sacred: your family, your comfort, your possessions, even your life! He demands it ALL! He likewise wants His followers to persevere to the end. He demands that we count the cost. No half-way or fair weather followers. He only wants followers who will follow for better or for worse.

Next, He tells an interesting story about a king who is at odds with a much more powerful king. I want to share some vital insight from this brief parable. The logical course of action in this scenario is to pursue terms of peace. That is unless you *prefer* certain destruction. Well, this matches our predicament with God quite strikingly. In our sin, we are enemies of God, lovers of self, the world, and Satan's allures, and our flesh is "king." We are pitted against insurmountable odds facing off against an omnipotent King. However, reality differs from the story just a bit—the powerful King has extended peace terms to us, rather than the other way around. We simply need to accept His terms and live at peace with Him.

You see, when the weaker force faces certain destruction, they have no bargaining chips. The powerful King sets the terms. God's terms are He will set us free from Sin and Death and empower us to walk in freedom from sin. We just need to surrender everything unconditionally and obey Him hence forth. Compliance leads to eternal life; failure to comply leads to Hell.

However, this is where it gets interesting, because the reformers did not accept His terms, but rather established terms of their own. Reformed theology goes something like this: we will accept His pardon, but we can not (and will not have to) obey His commands or necessarily surrender our lives to the King. What folly!

Throughout history, when people are subdued in battle, they are enslaved, their possessions are looted, and they are lucky if they keep their lives. Yet some think they can surrender to God and set their own terms of peace. All this while He has offered us peace with very clear, and I will say, very agreeable terms. God is not a tyrant, but He can (and will) subdue us either way. Yet He is offering us the choice to surrender voluntarily and be adopted as sons, or be subdued involuntarily and be punished as enemies of His Kingdom. Unfortunately, many haven't a clue what the terms of peace are, because false "terms" are promulgated by false messengers, as if they themselves were sent from the King's court. Yet all the while the King's true messengers have disseminated His true terms for all to see in the Holy Scriptures.

In the final verse of this passage, Jesus goes on to describe salt that loses its flavor. If Christians are salt and light, and some can lose their flavor, and it is called useless and to be thrown out, clearly this is reference to someone losing their salvation. I don't know how one could conclude otherwise.

Final Analysis

So what is the final analysis? The reformers would have us believe that Jesus died to satisfy God's wrath in a legal transaction, Jesus taking our place for our justly deserved punishment. In contrast, the early church taught that Jesus was sent to release us from the bondage of Sin and Death and turn our hearts back to God in repentance, following Jesus in loving obedience.

The reformers taught that we simply need to believe and we are saved into the pearly gates, unconditionally. The early church taught that we must repent and be baptized, fully surrendering our lives to Christ. By grace through faith we are saved—that is, grafted to the Vine. Yet that is just the beginning of salvation, the first step.

The reformers theology results in obedience to Christ being optional. Salvation is assured by faith regardless of how one lives. They go so far as to make doing good a bad thing by calling our righteousness filthy rags. (See Isaiah 5:20, Jude verse 4, and 2 Peter 3:14-18 for insight). The Scriptures and early church teach that our obedience to Christ's commands, in love, is required for salvation. It's not that we earn our salvation. Rather, our obedience is a direct reflection of our love and faith. We lie if we say we love and believe in Christ and do not do what He says. That's why Paul told us to "work out our salvation with fear and trembling" (see Philippians 2:12-13).

Likewise Peter said,

> For it is time for judgment to begin with the household of God; and if it begins with us first, what will be the outcome for those who do not obey the gospel of God? AND IF IT IS WITH DIFFICULTY THAT THE RIGHTEOUS IS SAVED, WHAT WILL BECOME OF THE GODLESS MAN AND THE SINNER." (1 Peter 4:17-18)

Now recall, the Gospel of God is to "repent and follow Jesus!" Modern Christianity leads us to believe that to get to heaven, we simply have to have the right theology and believe the right things, often independent of how we live. However, Jesus taught directly what the Judgment will look like:

> "But when the Son of Man comes in His glory, and all the angels with Him, then He will sit on His glorious throne. All the nations will be gathered before Him; and He will separate

them from one another, as the shepherd separates the sheep from the goats; and He will put the sheep on His right, and the goats on the left. Then the King will say to those on His right, 'Come, you who are blessed of My Father, inherit the kingdom prepared for you from the foundation of the world. For I was hungry, and you gave Me something to eat; I was thirsty, and you gave Me something to drink; I was a stranger, and you invited Me in; naked, and you clothed Me; I was sick, and you visited Me; I was in prison, and you came to Me.' Then the righteous will answer Him, 'Lord, when did we see You hungry, and feed You, or thirsty, and give You something to drink? And when did we see You a stranger, and invite You in, or naked, and clothe You? When did we see You sick, or in prison, and come to You?' The King will answer and say to them, 'Truly I say to you, to the extent that you did it to one of these brothers of Mine, even the least of them, you did it to Me.' Then He will also say to those on His left, 'Depart from Me, accursed ones, into the eternal fire which has been prepared for the devil and his angels; for I was hungry, and you gave Me nothing to eat; I was thirsty, and you gave Me nothing to drink; I was a stranger, and you did not invite Me in; naked, and you did not clothe Me; sick, and in prison, and you did not visit Me.' Then they themselves also will answer, 'Lord, when did we see You hungry, or thirsty, or a stranger, or naked, or sick, or in prison, and did not take care of You?' Then He will answer them, 'Truly I say to you, to the extent that you did not do it to one of the least of these, you did not do it to Me.' These will go away into eternal punishment, but the righteous into eternal life." (Matthew 25:31-46)

Sheep are not separated from goats based on their theology, what they believe, or whether or not they have faith. Jesus, being both the teller of the story, and the subject of the story says the sheep and goats will ultimately be separated based on how they lived—their fruit. The goats receive eternal damnation and the sheep eternal bliss based on what they did with their lives.

So who will you believe, the reformers or Jesus? If you answered Jesus, simply live out the Gospel according to Jesus: repent and follow Him! Go back and read the red letters again in light of everything we covered here, and simply obey what He said. Then reread the remainder of the New Testament in light of Jesus' Gospel. You will see incredible internal consistency in the entire New Testament with everything taught here. The scales will be lifted from your eyes and you will be free to follow Christ unhindered.